boards and asking styles

Initially, I took the Asking Style Assessment myself and found out I was a Mission Controller. I began to read specifically what steps I could take to be confident when I made an ask. The change in my own fundraising approach was so profound that I asked my entire board to take the Assessment, and we worked with Brian Saber until we all felt more comfortable speaking with donors.

Learning what each of our Styles was really helped us understand how to work together and how to make use of our diverse range of skills. One of my board members was a Rainmaker, and knowing that about her, we could pair her with a Go-Getter or a Mission Controller, like myself, to make a powerful asking team. Knowing our Styles helped us practice together, prepare better, and also understand and be sensitive to what kind of information our donor might respond to.

Our small arts organization's board launched its first capital campaign a few months after training with the Asking Styles. And we reached our fundraising goal shortly thereafter. As an Executive Director, there is nothing better than to work in partnership with a board on fundraising. It is an exciting and empowering process! And the Asking Styles are key to this partnership because board members can learn about using their natural strengths to build relationships and connections with donors.

Melanie Franklin Cohn
Former Executive Director
Staten Island Arts

boards and asking styles

a roadmap to success

brian saber

Boards and Asking Styles: A Roadmap to Success

Asking Matters
P.O. Box 1295
Maplewood, NJ 07040
www.askingmatters.com

This publication contains the opinions and ideas of the author. It is intended to provide helpful and informative material on the subject matter covered. It is sold with the understanding that the author and publisher are not engaged in rendering professional services in the book. If the reader requires personal assistance or advice, a competent professional should be consulted. The author and publisher specifically disclaim any responsibility for any liability, loss, or risk, personal or otherwise, which is incurred as a consequence, directly or indirectly, of the use and application of any of the contents of this book. No liability is assumed for damages resulting from the use of information contained within.

Printed in the United States of America

ISBN: 9798684903199

Book and cover design by Thomas Edward West of Amarna Books and Media
Photograph of Brian Saber by Colleen D'Alessandro

contents

dedication

This book is dedicated first and foremost to you, the board member. There are more than a million nonprofits in the United States alone, and every one of them needs a board. Add to that the countless nonprofits across the globe and that means millions upon millions of people like yourself are willing to give of their time and treasure to make the world a better place.

So much is asked of you and yet you rise to the occasion. You could use the time to play tennis or read a book, or spend time with your partner or family. You could use your expertise to advance your career or earn more money. You could use your treasure to take a vacation, have a great meal, or put away more for retirement. But you make a choice to share your resources because you care. You choose to use your time, expertise, and money for the betterment of the world. Thank you.

One of the reasons I've loved spending my life working in the nonprofit world is because of people like you. How amazing to always be surrounded by charitable, generous, caring people... people who share my passion for making a difference, for helping in some way, for understanding our privilege and sharing our resources.

Thank you for making my world so rich over the years.

foreword

Over the years I've seen nonprofit boards struggle in many ways—whether it's in working as a team, keeping their eye on the vision, delegating authority, respecting the professionals, or replenishing leadership. And as a lifelong nonprofit professional and consultant, I've worked with boards as they've strived to be effective, strategic fundraisers.

In these incredibly challenging times, good board leadership and resource development are more important than ever, and yet, in many ways, more difficult. COVID-19 has caused an unprecedented set of challenges in the modern nonprofit sector. Most boards cannot meet in person to conduct their work. They are left to manage the executive director remotely. Recruiting new board members is difficult for many reasons.

On the fundraising side, people are unsure about their futures and anxious about money. Meeting in person is extremely limited. There are far fewer opportunities for donors to see programs live and in action. And, for the first time, a wide range of organizations has had to trim their fundraising staffs. Under these circumstances, it's even more important to understand how the

Asking Styles can help you work productively and develop your organization's resources.

If you're like most board members, you've come to your current board with very little (or no) board experience and, even if you have experience, with very little board training. The same is true for your fellow board members.

The more you learn, and the more you can share with your fellow board members, the stronger you will be individually and as a team. And today that's more important than ever.

Brian Saber
President
Asking Matters

one

---

introduction

Being a board member is a noble effort. It can be incredibly rewarding, but also quite challenging. So much is asked of you in return for the wonderful feeling that you're making a difference in the world.

You probably already know our nonprofit world is quirky. In particular, the whole concept of nonprofit boards is weird. I could sugarcoat it, but the truth—as I've learned after working with hundreds of nonprofit boards—is that they're odd ducks.

Here's what I mean by that:

- On a corporate board, you're paid for your time, expertise, and legal responsibility. On a nonprofit board, you pay for the privilege of giving of your time and expertise, as well as accepting legal responsibility.

- On a corporate board, you give advice on how the corporation can make more money, and the CEO and their employees go out and implement those directives. On a nonprofit board, you do give revenue-generating advice, but you are also asked to help raise that revenue.

- Sitting on a corporate board is a plum job coveted by business executives and civic leaders. While sitting on some nonprofit boards offers cachet and connections, most nonprofits have to work hard to find a full array of solid board members and a few talented leaders. Then, board leadership and the staff have to do everything to entice board members to stay...and keep contributing and fundraising for that privilege.

It can all feel incredibly counterintuitive.

the goal

Almost every board member I've ever met has wanted to work hard and do the right thing. You are a noble lot. But that commitment and hard work have not, for the most part, been enough to build strong, cohesive boards that lead well and effectively develop resources for the organizations you love. And that's the goal—to lead well and effectively develop resources for your organization.

Leading well and developing resources enables your organization to have the biggest impact possible and fulfill its vision for the world. And that's what it's all about—impact and vision. You've come to the board because you're a believer. Most probably, a fellow board member or the executive director sat down with you and inspired you with their story of why they love your organization. They talked about the impact the organization is trying to make as it works to fulfill its vision for the world, and you got excited. You altruistically committed to giving your time and money.

Your fellow board members took the same path. You came together to make an impact...by leading well and developing resources.

And you can only do that by working as a team. Nonprofit board service is a team sport, where the entire board can only be as strong as its weakest members. When some board members are checked out, or unsuited, or don't feel validated, the whole board suffers, and the ability to lead the organization effectively goes out the door. The goal is to be a strong team.

the challenge

What could be so difficult? A bunch of committed, well-meaning people is tasked with a job that calls on all the skills you use in everyday life. You manage to be successful in your personal and professional lives. You interact with all types and you manage to deal with them. You make collaborative decisions with family, friends, and co-workers. You make things happen.

So why do boards struggle to hit their stride and be strong, effective teams? Because, as I noted, boards are odd ducks. Imagine a baseball team that:

- recruits players without experience and doesn't train them
- recruits players with experience and takes their word as to how effectively they played on their other teams

- convinces players to pay-to-play...and those who have more talent pay more for the privilege of playing
- is led by someone with few years of experience
- meets every two months to play and doesn't practice as a team in between

board dynamics are key

Given all this and much more, your board has to work hard to compensate for the natural inefficiencies and quirks of nonprofit governance. To do so, you and your fellow board members can benefit greatly from more fully understanding how your various personalities and working styles impact your ability to work together as a strong team.

When you understand these dynamics, you can tap into the full potential of each board member and the board as a whole. The stronger every board member is, the stronger the team will be. That stronger board will enable and inspire each board member to be more committed and engaged and, therefore, to play a bigger role in making an impact and helping the organization fulfill its vision.

The Asking Styles can help you achieve all of this, and this book will teach you how to get the most out of the Styles.

what's to come in this book

We'll start with an overview of the Asking Styles in Chapters 2 and 3. If you're already very familiar with them, you can jump to Chapter 4, where we'll talk about how to use the Asking Styles to understand what motivates board service for you. In Chapter 5 we'll discuss leadership. The Asking Styles of your board chair and committee chairs will impact how the board is run, and the makeup of your executive committee is particularly important.

In Chapters 6 and 7 we'll talk about using the Asking Styles to build the strongest team and, once you have, to keep everyone engaged and committed. The dynamics of board meetings are critical to this, as is everything your organization does in between meetings to strengthen the ties among board members themselves and between them and the organization.

Chapters 8 through 10 are all about being the best ambassador you can be. That starts with telling an authentic and compelling story. Once you're comfortable with your story, you can head out the door to represent your organization and help it develop important resources.

When it's time to recruit more great board members, the Asking Styles can be an important lens into how to build a well-rounded and balanced group. We'll cover that in Chapter 11.

Last but not least, in Chapter 12 I'll lay out some next steps.

Understanding your board through the Asking Styles lens will empower you and help you and your board be the most effective team possible. Imagine what you could then do to change the world!

two

asking styles
overview

In 2010, Andrea Kihlstedt and I founded Asking Matters. Our intent was to find a way to help board members feel more comfortable and be more effective fundraisers. What came out of that was the Asking Styles, which have become a staple of learning in the nonprofit world.

The Asking Styles have proved to be a powerful rubric through which to understand not only your strengths and challenges in cultivating and asking for gifts, but how you relate to your peers, how you can partner to be more successful, and how the Asking Styles of your board can significantly impact its ability to work productively and fundraise.

When it comes to fundraising, most board members—and the general public—have a stereotypical picture of a fundraiser. They see a hardcore salesperson always out to close the deal... someone who will do just about anything to get a "yes." And they say to themselves, "That's not me." Do you have this stereotype in mind?

The Asking Styles directly address and debunk this myth of the stereotypical fundraiser.

The Asking Styles are based on the concept that authenticity is key to building relationships. We can all successfully build relationships, and building relationships is at the core of fundraising. This means fundraisers must be true to themselves in order to be comfortable, confident, and effective fundraisers, and if you are true to yourself, you can be successful.

So, what are the key characteristics of an asker? I believe two predominate: how you interact and how you think. Let's explore them both.

how we interact

How we interact with others is at the root of all relationships. Some of us are naturally garrulous while others are quiet and more introspective. Some of us get excited when meeting new people, while others find it anxiety-provoking. Some of us do well in big groups and others shine in one-on-one situations.

Think of the last party or event you attended. Maybe it was one of your organization's special events. How did you feel? Were you excited to attend, or did you go because you had to? How did you behave at the time? Did you enthusiastically jump into and out of conversations, or did you find yourself huddled in the corner with one person?

And afterward, did you think, "Wow, I'm revved up...where's the next event?" Then perhaps you're an extrovert. Or did you think, "Get me home...I need to recharge." Perhaps you're an introvert.

People mistakenly think introverts don't like to socialize. This isn't the case. Introverts find great reward in their relationships with others, yet those interactions can often drain their energy, leaving them yearning to refuel with some quiet "alone time." This use of energy derives from the fact that introverts—myself included—think to talk. We like to stop and think about what we're going to say before actually saying it. We need that bit of time to process and formulate our thoughts. That bit of time might be a second or two, but it contrasts significantly with the extrovert, who talks to think.

Think back to that function you attended. Picture everyone milling about, coming in and out of conversations, and think of how rapid-fire the dialogue was. Did you feel you were in the mix, able to jump in and be heard? Or did it seem that every time you were about to say something—after pausing to think of what to say—someone else jumped in and you practically had to cut someone off to get a word in edgewise? If you were comfortably in the mix, you're probably an extrovert. If you were constantly frustrated or found yourself spurting out comments without enough thought, you're probably an introvert.

People always assume I'm an extrovert because I've mastered the art of conversation. They see me as confident and articulate and willing to engage those around me. What they don't understand is how much practice that's taken over my lifetime, and how much energy I expend in these interactions. Those who know me best know I turn down almost every party invitation...and every opportunity to meet new people. It just feels like so much work!

How we interact—where we are on the spectrum of extroversion/introversion—is the vertical axis of the Asking Styles:

extrovert = **derive energy from others** | **talk to think**

---

introvert = **derive energy from oneself** | **think to talk**

A word on the "spectrum": Try not to think in absolutes here. Many people believe they're not extroverts because they don't resemble some loud, overbearing person who monopolizes conversations and always hogs the attention (think Michael Scott from "The Office"). Or they believe they're not introverts because they assume introverts are hermits (think Shrek).

While some people certainly can resemble those caricatures, most of us are somewhere safely in between. That allows us to make our way in the world, interact positively with a wide range of people, and be successful in our work. We can draw on different parts of our personality at different times depending on the situation and the personalities of those around us. That doesn't mean we're trying to be anything we're not. We're simply reading the situation and acting appropriately and effectively in it. This ability we have to make our way in the world often leads people to confuse how we present ourselves with who we are intrinsically.

how you interact impacts how you fundraise

We know introverts aren't going to love their organizations' special events. These can be rather trying moments that we introverts tolerate because they come with the territory. As the extroverts jump into the fray (and we're so grateful to them for doing this!), we're likely to be found in a corner or along a wall. If we're lucky we'll wrangle one poor sucker to talk to us the entire time. I can't tell you how often I've only semi-jokingly offered my fellow staff a huge donation to our cause if I could skip one of these functions.

Our current virtual world doesn't help the situation. While introverts might more readily attend a virtual event because it provides some cover—it's easier to hide—they're also even less likely to interact. We all know how chaotic event video chat rooms can get. Imagine introverts trying to insert themselves into those conversations.

Putting special events aside, what does all this mean for cultivating and soliciting individuals face-to-face?

Extroverts—those who talk to think—tend to talk more readily and more often, while introverts—who think to talk—tend to talk more cautiously and less often. In a conversation, you're either talking or listening, so extroverts talk more and introverts listen more.

Coming back to the spectrum, if you're in the middle, the talking and listening might be very balanced for you. But what about the rest of us?

Extroverts open conversations easily—by phone and in person. Extroverts are much more comfortable picking up the phone to talk to a donor. They're more likely to use the phone to set up meetings and are adept at keeping the conversation on track and thinking quickly on their feet when the conversation goes off the rails. Introverts are more likely to send an email, as the pace of an email conversation gives us the time to think before talking. Email has been my best friend for almost thirty years, and I credit my success—and my having stayed in the field so long—to being able to use email rather than the phone.

In the solicitation meeting itself, extroverts excel at opening the conversation as everyone is settling into the meeting. Introverts need a few minutes to get into the rhythm, and this could mean some awkward gaps in the opening conversation.

Extroverts always have to remember not to dominate the conversation—especially if they're meeting with introverts. Their goal is to learn about donors by asking lots of questions, and they can't do that if they're spending the whole time talking. Since introverts think to talk, they naturally take the time to pause before speaking, which allows space for others to speak.

how we think

My three longest, most successful stints had one thing in common—bosses who just let me go out and do what I do best without a lot of analysis or planning. Ron Manderschied (Northwestern Settlement House), Nancy Winship (Brandeis University), and Janice McGuire (Hudson Guild) saw that I had the chops and the motivation to cultivate and solicit individual donors, and they knew instinctively that I wouldn't do well providing them tons of metrics. As long as the donors seemed happy and the dollars were coming in, they let me follow my instincts. For Ron and Janice, who were fellow intuitives, this was easy. For Nancy, this was a leap of faith, but she took the leap.

Intuitive people have gut feelings. Something in their head or heart says, "This is possible" or "This feels right." Based on that gut feeling, they act. They don't run the numbers or conduct deep analysis. They leap ahead. They act. And then they find out if their gut was right. Yet even this is based on intuition as they either sense they've made the right move or their gut tells them otherwise.

Analytics start with the data. They rely on charts, outcomes measurements, spreadsheets and other detailed materials and analyses. They pore over all the data and try to make sense of it. What are the trends? What story is the data telling us? Once they understand the data, they act on it, forming their strategies and plans. After taking action, they look to outcomes measurements to prove their actions are having impact. If the metrics don't add up, they'll analyze why.

How we think—where on the spectrum of analytic/intuitive we are—is the horizontal axis of the Asking Styles.

$$\text{analytic} = \frac{\substack{\text{inductive} \\ \text{fact-oriented}}}{\text{data to idea}} \quad \bigg| \quad \text{intuitive} = \frac{\substack{\text{deductive} \\ \text{idea-oriented}}}{\text{idea to data}}$$

how you think impacts
how you fundraise

Whether you're analytic or intuitive impacts why you care about your organization—perhaps what motivated you to join it in the first place—and how you talk about it.

Analytics are driven by the data. Whether it's a goal, a strategic plan, or just the facts and figures, this concrete and quantifiable information excites you and convinces you an impact can be made. In fact, without this information, the organization's vision is difficult for you to embrace. It will seem like pie in the sky and you're not likely to enthusiastically support it.

Intuitives are driven by an idea. You sense something—get something in your head or heart—and it drives you. You have faith in your gut and move ahead based on that. Perhaps you hear a story of a program participant whose life has been transformed, or you meet a staff member and are inspired by their work.

When we put the two axes together, we get the four Asking Styles:

Rainmaker: Analytic Extrovert
Go-Getter: Intuitive Extrovert
Kindred Spirit: Intuitive Introvert
Mission Controller: Analytic Introvert

Do you have a sense as to which Asking Style you are? Does one stand out? Or are you thinking more than one Asking Style could be you? This could very well be the case. As you'll learn, most of us have Primary and Secondary Asking Styles.

"Teaching the Asking Styles to our board and staff has allowed each of us to understand how we can have the most impact. We have learned to do what we do best. Our staff can now communicate better and team with our board in a more effective way. We have increased our success by bringing individual board members and staff members together with complementary Asking Styles. We have built a new leadership strategy with all four Asking Styles and built teams with complementary Asking Styles that are more effective communicators.

Our prospects now have the opportunity to hear our impact and vision as an organization with stories that come from a perspective of introverts, extroverts, analytics, and intuitives. We no longer tell one story from one perspective. The greatest impact is that each of us now feels empowered to work toward our goals using the best part of who we are. The Asking Styles is the breakthrough tool we needed to meet our goals as an organization."

—Mark N. Harvey, MD
Individual Giving Chair and Past President
Cystic Fibrosis Foundation, Sooner Chapter

three

the four asking styles

Let's walk through each Asking Style now. As you read the descriptions, think not only of yourself, but also your fellow board members. Who comes to mind? Later in the book we'll talk about how the various Styles interact and what this might mean for your fundraising and your teamwork.

Rainmakers

Analytic Extroverts: What's the Goal?

fact based
goal oriented
strategic
competitive
driven

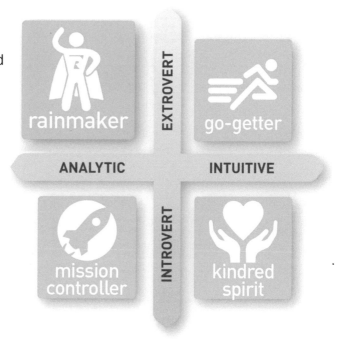

Rainmakers are the Analytic Extroverts. When people think of a fundraiser they think of you. They think of someone who confidently and objectively heads out the door to conquer the world and is strategically—and competitively—driven to achieve a goal.

When a Rainmaker is thinking through why something should matter, believing in the viability of a quantitative, aggressive goal is key. And you keep driving toward that goal, objectively. But it doesn't mean you solicit gifts at any cost; your every move is strategic. You are competitive and like to come out on top, and you get there by keeping your eye on the prize.

It's important to you to be well-informed and you'll take the time to pore through detailed information, including budgets, annual reports, outcomes measurements, and strategic plans. The more concrete information you have, the more compelling the case for support you can make.

Analytics are objective, following the facts. As someone who is extroverted and objective, you can be successful with a wide range of donors. You don't take things personally, and you evaluate everything through the prism of whether someone is or might be an important donor. Not taking things personally allows you to put rejection in its place. You clearly understand it's no reflection on you, but rather on where the donor is in their relationship with the organization and with their philanthropy. Further, you know their perspective might change over time, and you might even relish having to work a bit harder to get a gift. You're also willing to reach out to long shots and new prospects as you enjoy the challenge of turning them into donors.

...Does Rainmaker sound like you?

A few years back I led a webinar for the United States Olympic Committee's fundraisers from across the country. When I polled them on their Asking Styles, more than 90% identified as Rainmakers. I was taken aback until I realized many of them are current or former competitive athletes—of course they're goal-oriented and driven!

Go-Getters

Intuitive Extroverts: What's the Opportunity?

big picture
high energy
creative
quick
energetic

Go-Getters have an infectious, high-energy personality. You're passionate about the world and those around you, and you make friends quickly and easily. When I think of a Go-Getter, I think of the life of the party—someone who energizes a room, naturally links people together, and comfortably goes from conversation to conversation. Oh, and Go-Getters never arrive at a party until it's going strong! Are you nodding your head?

Go-Getters have gut feelings, and from that you develop a vision that you pursue confidently. While some of your ideas might fall flat, your willingness to take a chance and put yourself out there means that lots of great things can happen. And because you put it out there confidently, people are eager to follow along.

Your natural inquisitiveness serves you well. You love meeting with and learning about longtime and new donors alike. In fact, you're likely to befriend them over time.

And you're big fans of the interactive process. You love talking through ideas aloud and enjoy the back-and-forth debate.

In full disclosure, I love Go-Getters...until you guys drive me crazy! It took my co-founder Andrea (Go-Getter) and me (Kindred Spirit) a few years to figure out how to work together. We finally agreed that meetings should be no longer than about 45 minutes. Though she could be "in the moment" for hours, we found that my eyes glazed over after about 45 minutes and I could no longer hear/process anything she was saying.

...Do you think you're a Go-Getter?

For many years I worked closely with Judi Smith, the former Director of Planned Giving at the Arizona Community Foundation. Judi is a proud Go-Getter. Every time she asked me to send her information again because she couldn't find it, she said, "Don't you wish I had a little Mission Controller in me?" I told her I'd never sacrifice any of her big-picture thinking and infectious enthusiasm, and she could count on my Secondary Asking Style of Mission Controller (more on that soon) to keep us, and our work together, on track.

Kindred Spirits

Intuitive Introverts:
What Moves My Heart?

feelings oriented
attentive
caring
thoughtful
selfless

I'm a classic Kindred Spirit—an Intuitive Introvert. We're feelings-oriented and wear our hearts on our sleeves. Our decisions emanate from what we're feeling deep down. We use our gut just like Go-Getters do, but our choices come from a more emotional and personally reflective spot.

We take everything personally. Even after 35 years in the business, I still have to remind myself that whatever the donor decides is not a reflection on me. That it's always about where the donor is personally, charitably, and in their relationship with the organization—not about where they're at with me.

Being very sensitive ourselves, we Kindred Spirits tend to project that sensitivity onto others. We assume they're sensitive as well, and so we treat them with much attention and care. We're always asking people what we can do for them. We want them to feel good, to feel they've been heard and seen.

We try hard to avoid awkward moments, which can get in the way of best practice, which is to ask lots of questions and then ask outright for a gift. We worry about asking a question our donor feels is too personal or simply doesn't want to answer. And when we ask for a gift and the donor is ambivalent or pushes back, it feels like conflict.

Though our decisions are intuitive like those of Go-Getters, we don't make them as quickly. We appreciate the opportunity to take some time and consider our thoughts away from the pressure of an immediate response.

...Do you think you're a Kindred Spirit?

It took me 25 years to stop soliciting people I know well. It was always too personal, I couldn't separate their response from our relationship, and one day I decided the psychic cost—not to mention the small wedge I felt in our relationship—wasn't worth it. Recently I broke that rule and solicited a few close friends and family as I needed help supporting a young adult I was mentoring... and it only reinforced what I knew already about myself. I've now recommitted to not soliciting those near and dear to me.

Mission Controllers

Analytic Introverts: What's the Plan?

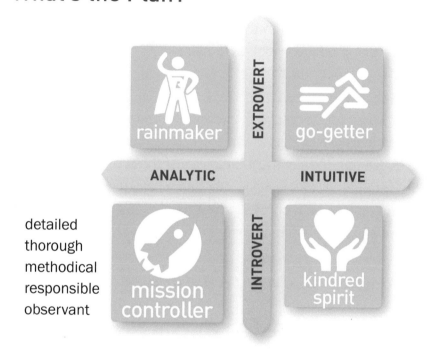

detailed
thorough
methodical
responsible
observant

Where would we be without Mission Controllers—the Analytic Introverts? Mission Controllers keep everything moving along when the rest of us might veer off course. You always get the job done.

Mission Controllers are detailed and thorough. You're great researchers, motivated to dig in and dig deep. And no matter how much research you do, you're likely to think there's more to be done.

You make decisions thoughtfully after reviewing all the available information. You're wired to ask for information in advance of meetings rather than being presented with it in the moment. If someone brings new material to a meeting, it can throw you off course as you know you won't be able to review it in detail before commenting on it.

Everything for the Mission Controller stems from a plan and the systems to implement it. Without a plan and systems, individual actions have no meaning or context. What good is a vision if there's no detailed plan to fulfill it?

Mission Controllers are great listeners—often the best listeners of all the Asking Styles. You're comfortable being quiet among others and enjoy the role of observer. When you do chime in, it will be with a well-thought-out remark. But people will need to make space for you and invite your participation, as you're not likely to jump into the fray.

...Do you think you're a Mission Controller?

Years ago I was interviewing a fellow fundraiser by phone. Each time I asked a question there was a long silence. Of course I wanted to fill it as it felt so awkward, but I learned I needed to give her the space to think through her response. She wasn't going to just blurt something out, but what she finally shared would be rich and detailed. Yes, she was a Mission Controller.

Having heard the four descriptions, which Asking Style sounds like you? Is there a clear winner? If not, don't worry. The Secondary Asking Styles will help you figure that out.

secondary asking styles

Are you thinking you're a little bit of this and a little bit of that? For most of us, even though one Asking Style stands out, we see a fair amount of another Style in us as well. Few of us fit neatly and completely in one quadrant or another. I call those who do the "uber-Rainmakers," "uber-Go-Getters," etc. The "ubers" are in the farthest corners of the grid, where both characteristics are equally, and significantly, dominant.

For most of us, one characteristic is more dominant than the other. Either our extroversion, introversion, analytic thinking, or intuitive thinking dominates. To reflect this, we also identify a Secondary Asking Style.

My Secondary Asking Style is Mission Controller, which means how I interact (my introversion) is more dominant than how I think. I need to constantly work through my reticence to meet new people, be part of group situations, etc. With my analytic Secondary Asking Style, my facility in numbers, calculations, facts, and figures complements my primary style that thinks from the heart and makes decisions based on gut. I've always loved math. I also have an interest in having things organized. My primary Kindred Spirit prefers that others do the organizing, but my secondary Mission Controller can make it happen if need be.

If your dominant trait is extroversion, you will find it interesting meeting new prospects and you'll find you can comfortably engage a wide range of people in a broad set of situations. You'll easily get conversations going and move them along, and these interactions will give you energy. However, you do have a tendency to talk too much, which is the kiss of death in fundraising as our goal is to listen and learn (more on that later). Your challenge will be keeping that in check and ensuring your prospects do the talking.

Not true for those whose dominant trait is introversion. You will excel at listening and giving prospects the room to speak. Since your natural tendency is to pause to think before talking, you create natural moments of quiet that your prospects can fill. And because your preference is not to be the focal point of a conversation or situation, you happily give that spotlight to others. Your challenges will be your limited desire to meet new people and the amount of energy those meetings take. You'll need to refuel often.

The analytic/intuitive dichotomy is also interesting. Analytic dominants will excel at internalizing the facts, figures, outcomes, and plans of the organization, and at sharing those compellingly with prospects. The intuitives will excel at creating and sharing inspiring personal stories—of your own journey and those of participants. Analytics will be challenged to find and share those stories, while the intuitives will find themselves working hard to embrace the organization's objective, factual information. We'll talk more about this when we cover developing your story in Chapter 8.

which do you think is your dominant trait?

If it's extroversion, you would be either:

    Rainmaker (Primary)/Go-Getter (Secondary)

    Go-Getter (Primary)/Rainmaker (Secondary)

If it's introversion, you would be either:

    Mission Controller (Primary)/Kindred Spirit (Secondary)

    Kindred Spirit (Primary)/Mission Controller (Secondary)

If it's analytic thinking, you would be either:

    Rainmaker (Primary)/Mission Controller (Secondary)

    Mission Controller (Primary)/Rainmaker (Secondary)

If it's intuitive thinking, you would be either:

    Go-Getter (Primary)/Kindred Spirit (Secondary)

    Kindred Spirit (Primary)/Go-Getter (Secondary)

[handwritten annotation: initial thought]

[handwritten annotation: survey response]

the asking style assessment

Are you ready to find out for sure? If so, it's time to take the Asking Style Assessment, a free 30-question, true/false assessment you can take online right now. The Assessment only takes three minutes to complete. Be sure not to overthink the questions (that means you, Mission Controllers!) Answer them based on your first thought. You will get a result immediately on screen, with a copy emailed to you. The result will include your Primary and Secondary Asking Styles and a description of your core strengths. To take the Assessment, go to:

www.askingmatters.com/find-your-style

Once you've taken the Assessment, come back to continue reading the book. We'll spend the next chapters talking about how to use your Asking Style to be the best board member you can be and to help build the strongest board team.

your results

So, what did you think? Did your Asking Style results match your original thoughts? Or were they different? Did the results change your mind?

Most people feel the results sum them up well. A few people have said they're not sold on the result they got. That may very well mean their true self is close to the origin of the axes:

If you're close to the origin, you've got fairly equal amounts of the various qualities that imbue each Style. This can be a great asset, as it may mean you're more adaptable to the various situations and personalities you'll encounter in your board work.

Don't worry if you're still unsure. Either choose a Style that feels a bit more like you than the others, or don't choose one and take away what makes sense from each chapter. You might find you've got a stronger sense of your Style after finishing the book.

your fellow board members' results

If your fellow board members are reading this book along with you, make sure everyone knows each other's results, as it will inform what you take away from the book. As you read it, you'll gain an immeasurable appreciation for your fellow board members, what they bring to the table, and how to work with them more successfully.

Even if you don't have everyone's results, you can make an educated guess based on how they interact, the questions they ask, the material they request, etc.

At the very least, keep in mind the board member you work with most closely (or your executive director), make an educated assessment about their Style, and ask yourself these questions:

- Looking back, how have our Asking Styles impacted our working relationship?
- How does their Style bring something to the table that I don't have?
- What can I do differently given their Style to improve our relationship?

EXERCISE: Asking Styles & Working Together

- Make sure everyone has taken the Assessment beforehand.
- Take 20 minutes at your next board meeting.
- Break into pairs and spend 10 minutes answering the following questions:
  ◊ What does one of us bring to the table that is helpful to the other?
  ◊ How do our Styles impact how we participate in group discussions?
  ◊ How can we work together more productively given our Asking Styles?
- Come back together and debrief.

"The Asking Style Assessment has been a very valuable tool in my board retreats to motivate greater board involvement in fundraising and outreach. While board members are generally responsible about their personal contributions, there is often a reluctance to engage in outreach and cultivation. The Asking Styles serve to increase their comfort level in outreach by acknowledging their differences and showing them that each can be effective in their own way.

I generally have board members complete the Asking Style Assessment prior to a retreat and bring in their report. They find the assignment interesting and there is a high rate of completion.

I then use the Assessment results as part of a discussion of cultivation techniques. Board members are divided into groups by their Asking Styles and asked to discuss the types of cultivation activities they would be comfortable with. As expected, when they report back, they find each group approaches the work differently. This helps them appreciate their differences as well as learn how to work together.

From here board members develop individual action plans that speak to their strengths, in addition to including techniques they heard from others that were also consistent with their Styles."

—*Michael Davidson*
Board Coach

four

your asking style and board service

Who you are impacts your journey as a board member every step of the way. From the beginning, it informs your worldview and your thoughts on how to make a difference. It impacts why you choose board service and your expectations for it. It impacts which organizations you choose to serve. It impacts how you experience board service.

Each of us is driven by how we view the world. As we walk through life, we see it through our unique lens. And that lens is molded by the key question driving each of us:

what's the goal? ... what's the opportunity?

EXTROVERT

ANALYTIC   INTUITIVE

INTROVERT

what's the plan? ... what moves my heart?

rainmaker board members: what's the goal?

Everything Rainmakers do is done with a goal in mind. So, when a Rainmaker decides to join a board, it's very purposeful. They may even set a goal of joining a board and then go out and find the right one. If an organization approaches a Rainmaker for board service, the Rainmaker thinks it through very carefully, asking lots of questions and looking for lots of data—measurements of the organization's outcomes in particular. They then sit down and decide whether serving on the board makes sense strategically in terms of what they'd like to accomplish.

The focus on metrics draws Rainmakers more to organizations whose programs lend themselves to analytics. For instance, if an organization is trying to reduce homelessness in a particular city by 10%, it either has achieved that goal or hasn't. A Rainmaker will strive to reach that specific goal. If an organization is advocating for the rights of the homeless in that same city, specific metrics may be more elusive, and that might be less inspiring.

Once a Rainmaker joins a board, the focus on metrics continues. This will give Rainmakers an important role in strategic planning as well as in program analysis. Nothing can be anecdotal here. Have we done what we set out to do? What do the numbers say? Are we doing more and are we doing it better?

The board meetings themselves can often challenge a Rainmaker...unless the chair is a Rainmaker! If not, the meeting might well be a bit less focused than is ideal. And forget meetings that start late or run late...or are long in general. Rainmakers, not being big on process, always opt for shorter than longer meetings.

go-getter board members: what's the opportunity?

Forget strategy, just bring on great energy and a sense of the future. What Go-Getters might lack in focus, they more than make up for in enthusiasm.

When a Go-Getter joins a board, it's because something excites them. They have a passion and joining a board helps them address that passion. If a Go-Getter is approached for board membership, talking enthusiastically about the opportunity to accomplish something great will stir them to action. They won't read lots of material or conduct a lot of due diligence. Their gut says either yes or no.

Go-Getters will be drawn to an organization focused on the future, just like Rainmakers. However, unlike Rainmakers their attraction won't be about strategy. Rather it'll be about their enthusiasm for the organization's grand and exciting vision. If the organization is metrics-based, that's fine, but the Go-Getter won't be watching those metrics along the way.

Go-Getters rally the rest of the team. Their passion rarely flags, and they bring great energy and lots of new ideas to a board. Some of those ideas fly, others don't, and sometimes they collide, but at least they're on the table and the organization can think big with a Go-Getter's input. And if enthusiasm around the board table is flagging, you can count on the Go-Getters to inject much-needed energy.

kindred spirit board members: what moves my heart?

Kindred Spirits share Go-Getters' intuition, but they act more on how they feel deep in their heart and on their compassionate empathy for others.

Kindred Spirits join boards because they want to help. They see a need and want to address it—in fact, they might feel a bit obligated to address it. They know they can make a greater impact by joining a board than they can on their own. As introverts,

Kindred Spirits' first inclination might not be to join a group, but they will make the trade-off in order to make a difference.

They are often drawn to organizations helping those in need, those organizations working to make the world a fairer place. If you reach out to a Kindred Spirit for board membership, share the most uplifting stories about the impact you're having—including stories of your beneficiaries' individual journeys.

With a Kindred Spirit at the board table, there's no chance of forgetting the "why." The Kindred Spirit will remind everyone that we do it because we care. We do it to improve life in some way for some group of people. The Kindred Spirit will be the one to point out that it might not be the best economic decision, but it can still be the right decision ultimately.

mission controller board members: what's the plan?

Goals are great; glad you see the opportunity out there; sweet that you care...but what's the plan? Without a plan, none of that matters.

Mission Controllers join a board to get the job done. And they know the organization can't get the job done without a solid plan that it sticks to. If we do A, B, and C, we can accomplish D. So when courting a Mission Controller, be careful of putting forth big, general ideas. Such nonspecific ideas translate to unrealistic and undoable. You've got to show them the plans, and the systems and methods you're using to make an impact. Show them the accountability—who's responsible for what—and the quantitative results to date.

A few years ago, I did a training for the fundraising staff of the Environmental Defense Fund (EDF). Everything at EDF is driven by science—by the facts—and they have detailed plans for how to address environmental issues to make a quantifiable impact. Not surprisingly, a lot of Mission Controllers are drawn to EDF, staff included.

Mission Controllers make it happen. Though they won't interject often at a board meeting, when they do they'll probe to understand if the idea is doable. They'll already be thinking about what's needed to succeed, which could be very helpful to the Go-Getter who has just proposed a pie-in-the-sky idea!

five

what's your board's leadership style?

It all starts at the top. Your board, like any group of people working collectively to the same end, cannot be strong without strong leadership.

Now let's see how the Asking Styles impact leadership at your organization.

board chair

Serving as a board chair requires a good deal of time and talent. An effective board chair can devote five to ten hours a week or more. Being a good leader means keeping your eye on the prize, delegating appropriately, creating unity, and much more. It requires a wide range of skills.

Every leader has strengths and weaknesses. No one has it all. The best leaders are self-aware and surround themselves with people whose skill sets complement theirs. Your board chair's Asking Style will give you a sense of their strengths and challenges:

Rainmaker
Role
- Keeps everyone's eye on the prize
Strengths
- Keeps everything moving toward your goals
- Pushes hard to succeed (themselves and everyone else)
- Approaches things objectively and factually
Challenges
- Not big on process and might not allow everyone to have their say
- Can forget to use their bedside manner

Go-Getter
Role
- Keeps the big picture alive
Strengths
- Has vision and gets everyone to buy into it
- Believes passionately
- Is very inclusive and encourages lots of process
Challenges
- Can be unstructured and not clear about where things are headed
- Has lots of ideas but doesn't always prioritize

Kindred Spirit

Role
- Remembers the people being impacted

Strengths
- Always keeps the beneficiaries front and center
- Makes sure all board members are heard and feel respected and appreciated
- Acknowledges everyone's efforts

Challenges
- Hard to discipline others and keep everyone in line
- Takes things personally and acts out of emotion

Mission Controller

Role
- Makes sure things are doable...and get done

Strengths
- Very planful and methodical
- Creates a sense of structure and forethought
- Listens to everyone's point of view

Challenges
- Can lose sight of the bigger picture
- Might not assert leadership when necessary

Years ago I had a board chair who was a Mission Controller. He was superb at keeping things moving ahead. Board meetings were organized and started and ended on time. Reports were submitted and reviewed. He did a great job of following Robert's Rules of Order. Yet he often got into the weeds too soon and, therefore, tended to give in to other board members' tendencies to bring the conversation down to an inappropriate level of detail.

Luckily, the former board chair, an active and formidable presence, counteracted that with his input at the table. He took big, calculated risks in life (do you hear Rainmaker?), knew the organization had to do so to have the greatest impact, and was the one to rally the troops through his confidence. He was also the one to say "Maybe that should be left to the committee" or "How about if the staff takes a crack at that."

EXERCISE: Your Board Chair's Asking Style

- Make an educated guess about your board chair's Asking Style based on the descriptions above.
- Ask yourself how their Style impacts their leadership and your working relationship.
- List three ways you might act going forward with this new understanding.

Depending on one's Style, each board chair will benefit from different leadership partners. As in most things, we often subconsciously surround ourselves with people similar to ourselves, yet what we often need is those whose talents are different but complementary. For example, if your board chair is a Kindred Spirit and the rest of your executive committee is as well, this will create a dynamic where everything is driven by the personal and it could mean important, objective decisions are hard to make. If everyone is a Go-Getter, you'll have lots of great ideas but might lack the framework to move them forward.

Now imagine the dynamic if you have a range of Styles on your executive committee. Imagine having various committee members who together make sure the board is strategically and systematically moving toward a vision while always keeping participants' needs in mind.

board committees

These descriptions hold true for your committee chairs and committee dynamics as well. Are you a committee chair and, if so, can you see where your Style impacts your leadership? What are the Styles of all your committee chairs and what can you infer from this? How about the committees on which you serve—what are the Style profiles of those committees?

I'm often asked whether one should assign committee leadership and membership based on Asking Styles. In both cases I think it should be a factor, but only after considering other factors such as leadership ability, subject expertise, and personal interest.

Example #1

Finance Committee Grappling With Fiscal Issues

Let's say your organization has had financial management issues—the books are a mess, you got a bad audit, expenses need to be trimmed, etc. This calls for detail people who will take the time to understand what's going on, come up with a plan to fix it, and stay on top of it while it's being addressed. Sounds like an extra helping of Mission Controllers is needed, though the other Styles would still provide balance (i.e., Go-Getters offering up outside-the-box solutions).

Example #2

Governance Committee Working to Enlarge the Board

Perhaps your board has dwindled due to natural attrition or a change in mission direction, and you need to quickly bring on new members to keep the board vibrant. This calls for outgoing people who will relish talking to people they may not know well, if at all, and getting to know them quickly. This might be an opportunity for Rainmakers and Go-Getters, the two extroverted Styles. Rainmakers will be more strategic in their work while Go-Getters will be best at just jumping right in and getting it done.

Example #3

Executive Committee Wanting to Improve Board Camaraderie

Is your board disjointed, with different camps or new members who don't know each other? Or perhaps you're a national or regional board that only meets in person twice a year and has to figure out other ways to develop board camaraderie. Or maybe our current virtual world is creating distance challenges. Kindred Spirits are always thinking of how to make others feel good and will enthusiastically dig into this project. They'll want to know what their fellow board members need to feel part of the team. You might add some Mission Controllers to implement the interactions once the Kindred Spirits have devised them.

Two final notes on this. First, getting board members to serve in leadership roles is not easy, and you might not have a lot of options or the ability to choose based on Asking Styles (or much of anything!). Often there is only one person who will take on a role, and that person might not even have the experience or talent necessary, in which case you work with what you have, understanding the strengths and limitations their Asking Style might bring.

Second, going through this analysis is not about scientifically placing board members in leadership roles, but rather understanding board dynamics and encouraging and supporting the best work possible. In some cases, it will give you "aha" moments, where you finally understand why something isn't working right, and you can make an adjustment. And it certainly can impact how you look at recruitment, which we'll discuss in Chapter 10. Some corporations use these types of personality "tests" when hiring, training, and promoting employees, and if you're with a large nonprofit you might be doing similar analyses. However, for most nonprofits the Asking Styles are a less formal but extremely helpful tool.

More than 30 years ago, I was brought on to the Chicago Dance Coalition board of directors as the treasurer because there wasn't an existing board member who they felt could do the job. A very unusual and risky move, but they decided my position heading a dance company and my finance background were enough of a credential and they had no other good options. Needless to say, I relied on my Secondary Asking Style of Mission Controller to do the job.

six

teamwork + camaraderie = synergy

Think of examples where you've been part of a team that has worked well together and whose company you enjoyed.

When a team is working well it feels good. You want to be a part of it. You're motivated to spend more time working together toward your common goals. Imagine the opposite, when you don't gel with the team. If you have to keep saying to yourself, "Well, I don't particularly care for so-and-so but he's doing a great job leading such-and-such," after a while it could sap your motivation.

Teamwork is key to a strong board. As board expert Michael Davidson says, "You can't do your job if you don't know what it is... and you won't do it if you don't think everyone else is doing theirs."

A board can't shine unless everyone feels they're in it together and everyone respects their fellow board members. This is especially true given the altruistic nature of a board, where you've come together for some common good. Yet this isn't always easy. Here you are, already giving so much of yourself, and now you're being asked to respect and value others whom you wouldn't choose as part of your inner circle...and to do so on a Monday night at a two-hour board meeting following a long day at work.

Knowing your fellow board members' Asking Styles will help you better understand their actions and better understand your differences. Keep in mind that you all approach teamwork from different perspectives and deal with teamwork differently:

- Rainmakers join a team because it's a strategic way to accomplish a goal. They feel the synergy of many people working together to form a solution. However, they come in with a very strong sense of what the solution or goal should be, and can bristle at the amount of group processing it can take to agree to a path forward.

- Go-Getters join a team because the interaction inspires them. They enjoy process and group discussion as it expands the mind and the possibilities. Yet that can often mean lots of ideas that may go in circles, or too many irons in the fire, which can leave the solution less strategically resolved than is ideal.

- Kindred Spirits join a team because they know it will be helpful to others. They'll listen to everyone and get along with the group, putting it first. However, when it comes to their own opinions, they often don't express them in the group because they fear a negative reaction, and that weakens the overall decision of the group.

- **Mission Controllers** join a team because it's the system through which a nonprofit advances its mission. They come to the table ready to listen and to help figure out how to make an impact. However, their overriding focus on the systems and details can frustrate others who want to keep the conversation at a higher level or explore other options.

These differences mean your board members will approach teamwork differently. The Rainmakers will push for shorter, more focused meetings while Go-Getters will enjoy open-ended discussions. Kindred Spirits will go along with what others want, even if it doesn't work for them. Mission Controllers will do their best to bring order to the proceedings.

camaraderie

Ca-ma-ra-de-rie (kämə'rädərē)—noun: Mutual trust and friendship among people who spend a lot of time together.

Does your board have a feeling of camaraderie? A board with camaraderie will work more cohesively and strategically. Board members will trust the work of committees and not micromanage committee decisions at board meetings. Board members will bring their best game to their work because they'll believe others are doing the same. And they'll do more for the organization.

The Asking Styles profile of your board will impact this camaraderie, and knowing your board profile will give you a sense of how to create it.

Everyone's voice must be heard and valued in order to create mutual trust and friendship. How do you accomplish that when everyone makes their voice heard a different way and needs to be valued in different ways?

Board meetings are where your board spends most of its time together, and if meetings are well run you can create tremendous camaraderie through them. You can also make a mess of them if they're not run right. I often think the number-one role of a board chair is creating camaraderie through board meetings.

board meetings

Now that you have a grasp of the Asking Styles, you're probably already having "aha" moments about how your board interacts. In board meetings, your extroverts—Rainmakers and Go-Getters— will be most vocal. They'll jump in when they have something to say...and take advantage of pauses in the conversation to say even more. Your introverts, by nature, will be quieter. They will offer much less of their opinion.

As an introvert, I rarely talk in large meetings. I often think, "I'll just share my thoughts privately at another time." This comes from a) feeling awkward when everyone turns to me to hear my pearls of wisdom, and b) thinking I can make my point more eloquently and fully without the pressure of the crowd (can you hear my Secondary Mission Controller in that?). I do much better if someone asks for my input, and the same is true in my personal life. I have a hard time asking for myself and always wish someone would just ask me to tell them what I want...or ask me 20 questions! Unfortunately, there isn't always that opportunity, so my voice sometimes doesn't get heard.

In our new virtual world, I find I'm participating even less in gatherings, both professional and personal. It's harder to get my turn without talking over someone. It's harder to feel the pauses in the conversation. And, with my mug up close and personal on everyone's screen, it truly feels as if all eyes are on me, which is uncomfortable.

And here's where your board chair is critical. It's up to your chair first and foremost to make sure everyone's voice is heard...and no one's voice dominates. That means working hard to manage discussions, and it can be as challenging to get your introverts to talk as it is to get your extroverts (especially your Go-Getters) to make room for others. It's also up to you and your fellow board members to value everyone's input and help ensure everyone is heard. Here are three ways to balance discussions:

- Ask for everyone's input on something. Literally go around the room and have everyone answer the same question. This is important even outside the context of a specific discussion item. Just asking everyone to say something ("Tell us why you're passionate about our organization" or "What's your why?") helps introverts start to feel more comfortable sharing their thoughts.

- Ask more reticent board members, in advance, whether they would share their thoughts during the meeting. This will give the introverts some comfort in doing so, as they can prepare ahead of time.

- Get introverts' thoughts in one-on-one conversations and then use what's learned to steer conversations and decisions.

Getting everyone's input is critical in making the best strategic decisions. But it's also critically important in making sure every board member is valued. Remember, just because someone doesn't speak up in a group setting doesn't mean that person doesn't want to be heard, and not soliciting their input could lead to their feeling devalued. Once that happens, there goes your camaraderie.

Who's most and least likely to share their perspective in a large group?

- **Rainmakers**—comfortable sharing ideas publicly and will keep homing in strategically with questions and observations.

- **Go-Getters**—comfortable speaking up and will take the conversation in various directions, not wanting to commit too early in the process.

- **Kindred Spirits**—will be slower to participate. Will prefer to share their thoughts at another time.

- **Mission Controllers**—will be reticent. Most likely to listen to everyone else, and then want time to synthesize that information and get further information, but might ask questions about execution.

---

building camaraderie through socialization

Camaraderie can develop outside the formal board or committee meeting setting. What opportunities does your board provide for members to get to know each other and interact beyond formal meetings?

Make sure you have time immediately before or after board meetings, as well as separately from board meetings (e.g., holiday parties), when board members can socialize with each other. You might ask people to come 15 minutes early for a toast to some success you've had. Or to meet a new board member before their first meeting. Perhaps your board chair will host an annual dinner or holiday party at their home or club, or at a restaurant? Or a few board members can take on the job of building board camaraderie and host casual gatherings throughout the year.

By now, even if you're not an introvert, you're saying to yourself, "Wait, won't the introverts dislike these larger social gatherings?" They might not always be as enthusiastic, but in many ways, these gatherings can help them. As they get to know their fellow board members better, their formal interactions will come easier. Still, be certain you're sensitive to your introverted board members and consider mixing in smaller gatherings. When I ran Hudson Guild, we set up small post-meeting dinners for four to six board members at a time. Given the board size and frequency of meetings, it allowed each board member to attend two of these each year. The dinners had no program or agenda, just the goal of building camaraderie.

When your board has teamwork and camaraderie, which of course feed on each other, it will have that special synergy that allows it to be extremely effective...and you and your fellow board members will relish your role and your work together. You'll listen more openly and respectfully to each other. You'll trust the committee work and the decisions emanating from it. You'll be willing to work harder. And that means a stronger organization that can have a bigger impact in the world.

seven

keeping everyone committed to the program

You and your fellow board members come to your organization excited about the work and the impact you can have. You're ready to dig in, be part of the team, and make a difference. Then the reality sets in. Lots of time in meetings, some of which might be a bit dull...or less productive than you hoped. Time away from family and friends. Conflicts with work. Financial expectations. Oh—and we need you to fundraise.

It's easy to lose that initial excitement and commitment to the work and, as in any relationship, the love tank has to be refilled.

The efforts your board makes to build teamwork and camaraderie help board members be vested. Yet to keep everyone committed and focused on the work, your board needs to go beyond teamwork and camaraderie and be proactive in regularly connecting to your organization's programs and activities. Again, the Styles can guide you.

Most board members need to connect to the program regularly to feel engaged. When they don't connect, the organization risks moving to the back burner. There are numerous ways to connect to the program, including:

- Visit programs
- Meet with program staff
- Have program participants or staff present at board meetings
- Represent the organization at events and meetings
- Read testimonials and stories
- Read program plans and reports
- Sit on the Program Committee

Let's discuss the first four.

visit your programs!

First and foremost is visiting the program in person, if at all possible. Nothing holds a candle to that, and I am always amazed at how often board members don't observe the programs they are committed to stewarding and safekeeping. While sometimes there are issues of distance (regional/national/international organizations), confidentiality (e.g., a counseling center), or safety (endangered or toxic lands), in most cases it seems to be more a matter of either benign neglect or competing time demands.

In this time of COVID-19, it's simply not possible for
many board members to visit programs in person,
so remote visits and other experiences will be key.
However, I've worked with many programs which can
safely host visitors—botanic gardens, preserved lands,
outdoor children's programs, sculpture parks, and
more—and board members will jump at the opportunity.

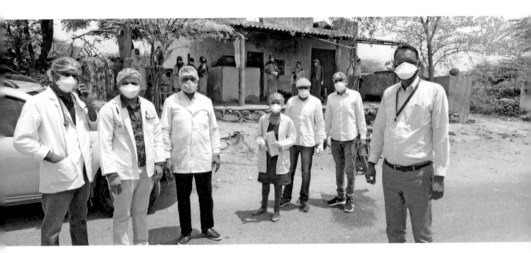

At Hudson Guild, we instituted a requirement that board members visit programs twice a year for half-day tours. They'd see
programs in action, meet with program directors, and tour the
facilities. I can't begin to tell you what an impact that had on our
board. Is it possible for your board to visit programs twice a year?
If not, what can you do virtually? Can you give board members
live tours of programs through a video chat or group Zoom call?
Imagine a virtual tour of a program where your program director
stops to talk to participants and board members hear firsthand
the impact the program is making.

Imagine how this might unfold based on Style. Let's say you and your fellow board members are on a tour of your pre-K classrooms. The Go-Getters are diving right into a big group of participants, eagerly volunteering to join in activities if appropriate. The Mission Controllers are hanging as far back as possible, waiting for the golden opportunity to learn more about how the work is accomplished. The Kindred Spirits have found one participant to talk to, learning about their unique experience. And the Rainmakers have made a beeline for the program director to ask lots of outcomes questions.

meet with program staff

When it's not practical to visit programs, it might still be practical to meet with program staff in person, or virtually. In these times, consider having regular (monthly) Zoom sessions where board members can chat live with a program director and/or their staff. If you're meeting virtually, remember to make space for the introverts to ask questions and have their opinions heard.

And, where appropriate, have a subgroup, or even an individual board member, meet with program staff separately.

have program presentations at every board meeting

Without exception, every organization should have a program presentation at every meeting. Period. No excuses about time and logistics. I've never attended a board meeting that didn't fritter away 15 minutes or couldn't be extended by 15 minutes. If you're looking to find time, it's a great excuse to move to a consent agenda (one where all committees submit reports in advance and committee chairs only present when discussion or a vote is needed). By the way, consent agendas have numerous other benefits, such as keeping the board from second-guessing the decisions of their fellow board members.

Here's a tip: have your program presentation at the top of the meeting. It will excite your board members, helping them to get behind bigger ideas and helping them put the meeting's discussions and resolutions in proper perspective.

represent the organization

Serving as an ambassador and advocate is one of your most important roles. This is particularly true for small and midsize organizations, where there are often more board members than there are staff. You can vastly multiply the organization's visibility footprint by being an active spokesperson at:

- Site visits with funders
- Fundraising meetings with individuals and institutions

- Special events of all kinds
- Advocacy meetings
- Sector networking events
- Community events
- Staff functions

Again, think of the Asking Styles. While almost every board member can be an asset in a small group setting, some of your board members will be better matched for the larger events. Further, sometimes you will want the passion of a Go-Getter and sometimes the strategic focus of the Rainmaker, and so on.

Let's never forget: no matter how committed you are, you have a life outside this organization you love. You focus for a bit and then go back to the rest of your life. And even within the organization, the focus can become quite narrow and mundane. Reconnecting to the program reminds you of the "why"—why you work so hard for the cause.

eight

telling your story

Besides commitment and passion, the key to your success is being able to tell your story—to make your case for support. With a compelling story, you can be a superb ambassador and advocate. You can excite and entice others to help the cause you love. And while fundraising is essential—every nonprofit needs funds—your role is much broader than that. Resource develop-ment means everything from finding those with specific expertise to serve on committees and give advice, to finding in-kind products, to getting others to serve as advocates.

I often observe board members afraid to talk on behalf of their organization because they don't think they know enough to be articulate. They witness staff talking eloquently and think, "I can't do that. I don't know all that stuff." Is that you? Well, the truth is you don't have to be as eloquent as staff...and you don't have to know everything. No one expects that of you as a volunteer. If you tell a passionate story about why you care and are involved—a story that is compelling to you and authentic to who you are—that story will resonate with everyone. And those you're cultivating will then ask you questions...which you may or may not be able to answer. And that's OK!

It must be a story told passionately and authentically, and that will only be the case if it's a story based on what moves you. It can't be your organization's "elevator pitch," something every board member is expected to recite to everyone they meet. If it's that generic, you won't sound authentic unless you've got great acting chops. It will also be hard to deliver the "pitch" passionately. Neither of these will entice the donor to build a relationship with you and the organization.

I've been asked countless times, "Don't I need to tell people what they want to hear?" Yes, but what people want to hear is your passion and authenticity. If your presentation doesn't touch on everything someone is curious about, they'll ask you questions. Those questions will be very enlightening and help you better understand the donor's interests. And, frankly, this idea of trying to tell donors what you think they want to know is a bit of a red herring.

How often do we really know in advance what someone wants

to hear? Much less often than we'd like. That assumes they've given us lots of their time, which often doesn't happen.

Though your story should be your own, the best practice is for you to focus on vision and impact. While it's often easier to talk about the organization's needs, gifts in support of vision are bigger. When your donors are asked to support a need of your organization—such as more space for programming—they'll contribute something. We're a caring society and people respond when asked to help. But gifts of need are small. Gifts of need are bandages on a wound.

If you talk about the vision your organization has for what it can accomplish with more space, people can see themselves partnering with you to fulfill that vision. The gifts they ultimately make will feel like investments in a better future. And gifts that feel like investments will be larger.

How about impact? Do you find yourself reciting a litany of deadening facts, such as 500 meals a day for seniors, four state-of-the-art science labs, a new bus with interactive exhibits, etc.? These are the features of your organization. As proud as you are of those 500 meals, what's more impressive is the impact you have on seniors because of those meals. Ask yourself what the benefit of serving those meals to seniors is and what the impact of that benefit is. How are those meals helping your organization change the world?

So, your story must strive to talk about vision and impact.

Yet that doesn't mean every story must be the same. Based on your Asking Style, you're going to use a different vocabulary to describe your organization's vision and impact. You're going to tell a different story about those meals for seniors. Let's think back to that core question that drives you forward:

what's the goal? rainmaker EXTROVERT go-getter what's the opportunity?

ANALYTIC INTUITIVE

what's the plan? mission controller INTROVERT kindred spirit what moves my heart?

Rainmakers will use facts and figures, outcomes, goals, and strategies to tell a story. You will tell a "goal story." Here's your Rainmaker version:

"I'm so excited by our work with seniors at Allenville Senior Center. Our goal has been to decrease isolation and increase nutritional intake among seniors in our community so they have a better quality of life in their later years. By providing breakfast and lunch to seniors five days a week, we are impacting their lives in just a few weeks. Within a month of joining our Center, 75% of seniors self-report significant decreases in their feelings of isolation, and our registered nurse reports an almost complete elimination of the insidious weight loss these seniors often face when they're responsible for their own meals. One of our clients, Lucinda, self-reported that in the month she's been with us she has had significant decreases in her feelings of isolation, and she hasn't lost a single pound!"

Go-Getters have the easiest time talking in a visionary way. You comfortably talk about the big-picture possibilities, so building the case for support comes naturally to you. Here's your "opportunity story."

"I'm so excited by our work at Allenville Senior Center. Imagine what the world would be like if we could keep all seniors in society from any unnecessary decline in their later years. Well, here at Allenville we've come up with a solution for our community's seniors. By offering them breakfast and lunch every weekday, we've found it's possible to significantly decrease their feelings of isolation, and at the same time we get them all the nutrients they need to maintain their weight and their health. One of our clients, Lucinda, self-reported that in the month she's been with us she has had significant decreases in her feelings of isolation, and she hasn't lost a single pound! We're impacting lives such as Lucinda's in profound ways."

Kindred Spirits are more likely to talk about mission—"our mission is to ..." And if anyone is going to weave in personal stories of program participants, or tell their own story, it's a Kindred Spirit. You'll tell a "heart story."

"I'm so excited by our work at Allenville Senior Center and I'd like to share a story. Lucinda joined our senior center a month ago. When she first came, she was feeling completely isolated due to very limited human contact, and she was depressed that her life was so solitary. We also found that when she was living by herself, she had been losing weight because she wasn't cooking well for herself and regularly skipped meals. Obviously, her depression added to her lack of desire to eat. This is a story we hear time and again, and it breaks my heart to think these seniors—people's parents and grandparents—are in such dire straits. Since coming to Allenville, Lucinda has self-reported significant decreases in her feelings of isolation, and she hasn't lost a single pound. And this is true for the hundreds of seniors we serve every day."

Mission Controllers will talk about the methods, systems, and plans used to have an impact and fulfill the organization's mission, because without a roadmap to get there, the end goal will never feel real to you. You'll tell a "plan story."

"I'm so excited by our work at Allenville Senior Center, where we are directly addressing the issues of isolation and nutritional deficiency. We developed a program to identify at-risk seniors that includes home visits and checkups. We enroll them at Allenville and a registered nurse does an intake to record their feelings of isolation, their weight, and other vitals. We then provide them breakfast and lunch five days a week. Through our work, 75% of seniors self-report significant decreases in their feelings of isolation, and our registered nurse reports an almost complete elimination of the insidious weight loss these seniors often face when they're responsible for their own meals. One of our clients, Lucinda, self-reported that in the month she's been with us she has had significant decreases in her feelings of isolation, and she hasn't lost a single pound!"

If you make the story your own and tell it passionately and authentically, you will be a superb ambassador and advocate for your organization.

EXERCISE

- Write out 200 words in response to "Tell me about your organization."
- Circle any references to vision and impact.
- Make a mental note of whether your response reflected your Asking Style.

"Asking Matters and the Asking Styles helped me to create a culture of philanthropy at my organization by allowing the board to lean into who they are and use it to help tell the Esperanza Academy story. By coming to understand them through their Asking Style, our staff and volunteers are now able to be great ambassadors and connectors with authenticity and confidence."

—*Gia Angluin, Director of Development*
Esperanza Academy, Lawrence, MA

nine

getting appropriate material support

I distinctly—and painfully—recall giving every board member a folder with what I deemed important information. This included strategic plans, financial reports, press clippings, and such. Yet I never thought of how individual board members best learn, and I certainly never thought about what would inspire each of them—what would keep their commitment and passion alive and help them tell their story. Some board members will read everything they're sent. Some will pore over financials, as it's the numbers that tell them the story. Some will crave the visceral feeling of seeing the program in action and speaking to participants if possible, and will only glance at written materials. Think of significant gifts you've made in the past and what you wanted to know before making those commitments.

Here's the Asking Styles roadmap to getting the support you need in order to play your ambassadorial and resource development role:

facts and figures
strategic plans
budgets
outcomes analyses

EXTROVERT

rainmaker   go-getter

ANALYTIC   INTUITIVE

INTROVERT

mission
controller   kindred
spirit

plans
budgets
annual reports
program statistics

vision statements
stories
one-page fact sheet
talks with staff

mission statement
stories
one-page fact sheet
visits to programs

rainmakers—what's the goal?

Since Rainmakers are driven to reach a goal and measure their success that way, it's critical that they review material that shows progress and achievement, and the strategy behind it. This material must be quantitative, as Rainmakers are analytic. This means digesting the strategic plans that prove ideas have been well thought out, and poring over the financials, analyses, and outcomes measurements that prove the plan works.

Imagine a Rainmaker trying to make a strategic, goal-oriented decision for your organization without the backup material. A Rainmaker will never vote to expand programs without proof that existing programs have been effective, and that proof can't be anecdotal.

go-getters—what's the opportunity?

As intuitives, Go-Getters have a gut feeling that some direction or idea is right, and they go for it with confidence and gusto. Once they have an idea in their mind, they don't need much convincing, so once they've bought into your organization's vision, they're all in.

Go-Getters crave inspiring stories and hearing about the organization's vision from leadership. They enjoy meeting with program staff who can inspire them further about the impact the programs are making. They won't want to be bogged down with lots of material—everything should be in summary form so it's actually read! Facts should be kept to a minimum—what fits on one page? Might the strategic plan have an executive summary?

kindred spirits—what moves my heart?

Kindred Spirits are driven by emotions. They act out of concern and a sense of responsibility. They want to do the right thing. As intuitives, they feel it in their gut, but they're also open to hearing it from others.

Nothing will move Kindred Spirits more than meeting with the beneficiaries of your programs. While all board members should interact with programs (staff and beneficiaries), it is particularly critical for Kindred Spirits. If logistics or privacy issues stand in the way, Kindred Spirits will enjoy video testimonials or anonymously written stories. As with Go-Getters, facts are less critical with Kindred Spirits, and while they might read everything out of a sense of obligation, it won't inspire them and might overwhelm them, so keeping it brief is good.

mission controllers—what's the plan?

Without a plan, nothing is possible for Mission Controllers, and a set of ideas and goals is not a plan. A plan is thought out, methodical, and detailed. Once Mission Controllers have confidence that the plans are sound, they'll be inspired to go out and sell them enthusiastically.

While strategic plans are well and good, it's the business plan with all the action steps and deadlines that is most important. No amount of detail is too much for Mission Controllers, who are the most likely to feel they still need to know more before heading out. They'll read every budget line item, note and report, and all the statistics that back up the plan.

ten

---

resource
development

How many board prospects have said to me over the years, "I'll do anything but fundraise." I'm sure you've heard that...or said it yourself. And it's no wonder, since most people assume board fundraising means hitting up everyone they know...and then contributing to their donors' charities. Further, chances are you've never been given any training, so you have no idea what good fundraising entails.

While it's great if you and your fellow board members bring a network, not all will, and it's not imperative that you do. What is imperative is that all board members help in resource development. And resource development is much more than asking for money. Your organization needs a full array of resources, and you can help develop them:

- In-kind products and services
- Outside expertise
- Someone to open a door
- Non-board committee members
- New board members
- Visibility
- Places to hold meetings and events

Further, when developing these resources, much more time is spent cultivating people than soliciting them. When we're developing resources strategically, we're spending almost all our time cultivating donors by:

- Educating them about what you do
- Educating them about the impact they can have or have had
- Thanking them for the resources they've provided
- Making them feel appreciated and important
- Making connections to others who are involved with your organization

who to cultivate and solicit

You and your fellow board members will approach your circles of influence differently, and it's not only based on what that circle of influence is. It's equally influenced by your Asking Styles:

Rainmakers approach their contacts strategically, and are most likely to tap their professional network. They think through those relationships, what the "sell" is, and what influence they have.

Go-Getters cast the net wide, given their boundless enthusiasm. They take an "all for one, one for all" approach and try to bring everyone into their world. They often succeed due to their positive energy and creativity.

Kindred Spirits avoid those closest to them at all costs. Kindred Spirits also can be shy or anxious meeting new people, so we do best with those we know but with whom we're not particularly close.

Mission Controllers approach their contacts systematically. They'll come up with a plan, start with a specific group, and work out from there. They cast the net wide like Go-Getters, but much more methodically.

What about prospects from your organization's database? Board members can often be even more helpful working to cultivate and solicit your organization's list, and for many board members it's much less stressful doing so than approaching their own network:

new donors
Rainmakers and **Go-Getters** are most likely to agree to cultivate new prospects—those who haven't given or those who have given but are unknown. Their extroversion minimizes their discomfort in new situations. Further, your Rainmaker board members like the challenge of turning a prospect into a donor... and the Go-Getters just love meeting new people.

longtime donors

Kindred Spirits will be most comfortable when there's familiarity and less rejection to fear, so I often assign these donors to Kindred Spirits. For instance, with longtime donors the question is often more about how much they'll contribute rather than whether they'll contribute at all.

foundations

Mission Controllers are a great match for foundations—both institutional and family-run. Foundations are more structured and formal in their philanthropy than individuals, and Mission Controllers work well within that framework. Additionally, meetings with foundation officers tend to be straightforward and predictable, which Mission Controllers appreciate, as it can be difficult for them to be thrown a curveball after all their planning and preparation.

donors with the most potential

Rainmakers will be driven to succeed and motivated by the fact that the gift is so large, whereas others might be intimidated by the magnitude of what's at stake.

planned gift donors

Kindred Spirits are most likely to be sensitive to donors' wishes and to overall discussions of legacy giving. They'll be deferential and supportive, giving donors comfort during these often sensitive discussions.

corporate sponsors

Rainmakers will best convey the benefit your organization's sponsors will receive by underwriting programs, events, etc. And they'll appreciate the let's-get-down-to-work attitude corporate representatives bring to meetings since Rainmakers are not big on process. **Mission Controllers** will have done their homework, understanding most completely the corporation's culture, interests, and guidelines. And they'll do best at conducting orderly, businesslike meetings that follow an agenda.

lapsed donors

Go-Getters might do best given their innate enthusiasm, which could inspire lapsed donors to come back into the fold.

what types of cultivation you'll like... and execute best

Board members' Asking Styles will help determine the types of cultivation activities that work best for them, and how they navigate those which are less comfortable.

Let's talk about fundraising events. First of all, it's probably your extroverted board members who proposed you have them. Most Kindred Spirits and Mission Controllers can live without them! Given that, when it comes time for fundraising events, lean more heavily on your Rainmaker and Go-Getter board members to cultivate event attendees.

Cultivation events are a different story. They succeed as much based on one-on-one conversations as they do on the presentation and the energy in the room. Kindred Spirits and Mission Controllers are in the zone when they can focus on one person... and in a setting where things aren't in a huge swirl of people.

Having said that, Kindred Spirits and Mission Controllers will still prefer one-on-one meetings, such as showing a single donor around your program, or meeting over coffee or a meal.

Rainmakers will excel at local business networking events where they can make their own connections as well.

Go-Getters will excel at leading individual and group tours of your organization's programs, introducing donors to staff, etc.

Kindred Spirits will excel at taking donors out for coffee, visiting their homes, and thinking up special ways to acknowledge them and make them feel important.

Mission Controllers will excel at keeping on top of everything and continuously moving relationships ahead while providing detailed material at all times.

Thank-you calls are a wonderful way for board members to serve as ambassadors and resource developers. Go-Getters are best at the calls, as they're most comfortable just picking up the phone in the moment and conveying their enthusiasm. Rainmakers find picking up the phone easy, but don't expect them to spend much time on those calls! Kindred Spirits and Mission Controllers will struggle with the phone, so be very careful about who you assign to them.

partnering

Partnering to cultivate and ask for gifts is incredibly effective. I'm a big fan of partnering and would rather focus on fewer donors and deeper relationships when I'm marshalling everyone's time. Multiple relationships with donors can also provide more consistency over time. Further, as you and your fellow board members grow into your fundraising roles, partnering can also serve to give you comfort and training. Consider going out in pairs or pairing with staff.

All things being equal, see if you can pair according to Asking Styles. If you partner diagonally, you will have covered all the bases. If the donor is more analytic, the Rainmaker or Mission Controller can take the lead. The same is true for intuitives (Go-Getters and Kindred Spirits). The extrovert and introvert will also complement each other well.

training and practice

You and your fellow board members need to be trained and then practice what you learn in order to tell your story, open doors, have meaningful conversations, ask great questions, and solicit support. Getting that training and practice can be challenging and, no surprise, your Style will dictate what's best for you.

Boardwide training should be a given. Taking time offsite—or at least out of the regular rhythm of board meetings—is paramount.

You might have an able facilitator among your peers and staff, or you might bring someone in. It will be money well spent.

However, keep in mind what we've talked about in terms of group dynamics. Some board members will thrive in a group training session. Others will participate but might need some guidance or support.

Besides the fact that training/practice must be ongoing, it also needs to be rich in variety. Based on Style, some board members will learn best one-on-one, and some will want to watch videos or participate in webinars. Others will want to write out detailed notes and then pose questions to an expert. Make sure your organization offers various opportunities, and on a regular, ongoing basis.

I do recommend group trainings—even though some board members would prefer to avoid them—as they are important team-building opportunities. However, that means being aware of the strengths and challenges everyone brings to the room and creating a safe, supportive environment.

Resource development is a critical role for you and your fellow board members. Your organization needs your assistance to find the resources to fulfill its vision and have its greatest impact. It's not easy work, but if you get proper training and embrace your Asking Style, you can make a difference.

EXERCISE: Partnering and the Asking Styles

- Choose someone you partner with or would like to partner with to cultivate and/or solicit a donor.
- Take a guess as to their Style.
- Ask yourself two questions:
  - How do we complement each other?
  - What might our #1 challenge be working together?

eleven

---

recruitment

In Chapter 3 we talked about the Asking Styles profile of your board. What did you find is in short supply? Where are you imbalanced? If you had your druthers, who would you recruit?

I know boards often think of filling board slots based on expertise, such as financial, marketing, or real estate, or based on leadership potential. And these needs are real. But to the extent possible, it's also important to recruit based on creating a strong team that works together well. As I noted earlier, this isn't always possible. Often board membership is a seller's market—we need board members more than individual board members need our particular organization. But where we do have options, using the Asking Styles can be a helpful lens.

Let's assume you know you need more Mission Controllers, Go-Getters, etc. How do you figure out the Asking Style of a board prospect as a way of understanding how that prospect might fit into the board's culture?

The easiest way is to ask board prospects to take the Asking Style Assessment. If you have an intake form (highly recommended), reporting back one's Asking Style can be part of the process. You can even ask board prospects to share what they learned from taking the Assessment and how they think that impacts what they would bring to your board.

If you can't ask them to take the Assessment, you can still ask them helpful questions during the interview process. Here are some that would be quite revealing:

- What do you find most compelling about our organization and why?
- How do you make decisions?
- What experience do you have working as a group and what do you find most inspiring and most challenging in that setting?

Let's take the first one as an example:

"What do you find most compelling about our organization and why?"

- "I was wowed to hear you've increased reading scores by three levels in one year."—Rainmaker
- "I can see where the literacy work you're doing will mean

these kids have much better lives."—Go-Getter
- "I want to help these kids as it's awful how far behind they are, no fault of their own."—Kindred Spirit
- "I love the system you've got in place. It makes sense that you have these teams to support each kid individually."—Mission Controller

Here are other ways to get a sense of the Asking Style of your board prospect:

Rainmaker
- Will ask to see all your financials
- Will keep meetings short and want to get to the point
- Will be most interested in an organization that is really striving hard to grow and make a bigger impact
- Will ask lots of questions to dig deep and make sure things add up

Go-Getter
- Won't ask for much information
- Will be very enthusiastic about the big picture
- Will happily meet and spend time
- Will ask lots of questions out of curiosity

Kindred Spirit
- Will be deferential
- Won't ask lots of questions
- Will accommodate your schedule
- Will be moved by very personal stories

Mission Controller
- Will ask for operating plans
- Will ask questions about how things are accomplished
- Will be quieter and might come off as shy or retiring
- Will pause before answering questions

appreciating group dynamics

Serving as a board member isn't for everyone. It isn't for lone rangers, grandstanders, or know-it-alls. It isn't for those who don't understand group dynamics and don't have respect for the "all for one and one for all" nature of boards. Have you ever thought to yourself:

"I don't know why so-and-so joined our board..."

"...they seem frustrated and they keep causing unnecessary issues."

"...they don't come to meetings and don't seem to understand how important it is that they do."

"...they seem uninterested in others' opinions."

Figuring this out in advance can save you and the board prospect a ton of angst and frustration. So consider posing one of these hypothetical questions:
- We're facing a painful budget shortfall this year because our gala came up very short and we lost an important contract. We're looking at having to curtail services. How would you like to see this issue addressed by the board?
- We're two years into a five-year strategic plan and the results aren't there. Many board members feel that's on the executive director and have concerns that he isn't the right person for the job. What should the board do?

These situations are perfect examples of board-level issues, and the answers will be very telling. Besides answering based on Style, you'll get a sense of your board candidates' appetite for group process. We know Go-Getters will enjoy it. Mission Controllers, while not big on group discussion, will appreciate the process. These situations are harder for Rainmakers, who aren't big on process, and Kindred Spirits, who aren't big on group discussion. And that's OK, as long as they can still respect the process and understand the need for it.

Further, though I've talked about people of various Styles being attracted to different organizations, in fact it is often those less aligned by Style who are most needed. Since we naturally gravitate toward those more similar to us, and people naturally gravitate to situations that feel more comfortable than less, boards can become a bit homogeneous over time. When that happens, the discussion gets stale and important pieces go missing. With a rich mix of board members, you're sure to have strategy, opportunity, heart, and plan sitting around the table.

twelve

---

next steps

Now that you know your Style and how it impacts you, here are some next steps to take:

Make a few brief lists to help you remember key points
- The top five things I've learned about myself
- My top three strengths as a board member
- My top three challenges as a board member
- The three things I will do differently now

- The three board members who challenge me most and what I now understand about them

Have a discussion with a fellow board member

Ask a fellow board member to read this book and then sit down over coffee to share your insights:

- What did we learn?
- How might we work together given our Styles?
- How do we see our board through this new lens?
- What recommendations might we make to board leadership?

Take advantage of various Asking Matters resources at www.askingmatters.com

- Sign up for my free newsletter to get monthly advice and announcements.
- Check out my free videos for thoughts on more than 20 topics.
- Join me for my free Fundraising Masters webinar series to learn from my favorite experts in the field.

developing your organization's strongest board with the help of the asking styles

Developing your strongest board is an ongoing process. I always recommend looking at a three-year horizon. Can you envision your strongest board? What does it look like?

Even if you feel you have an incredibly challenging board and can't imagine it working well, keep in mind that in three years...

- Many of your current board members will have been inspired by the new direction and new understandings and have risen to the occasion.

- A few board members will have realized they don't fit in given the new direction and will have left the board.

- A few board members won't have grown and will be unhappy, but they will have stayed because they couldn't bear to leave.

- All your new board members will understand the new direction and be completely on board (pardon the pun!).

So where do you start? Since some group of people needs to spearhead the change, figure out which existing team makes the most sense for you. Depending on your organization's unique character and the pieces of the board puzzle you want to work on most, one or more of the following teams will be the right place to start. Which of these teams is working effectively or seems to be best positioned to use the Asking Styles in discussion, for training, for improving board dynamics, and more? Perhaps more than one team can take on the work:

executive committee

This is always the best place to start, if possible. These are the leaders who set the stage for the whole board and are overseeing how the board operates, what roles everyone plays, what gets onto the agenda, etc. The Executive Committee can:

- Decide how to incorporate Asking Styles discussions and exercises into board meetings

- Use the lens of the Styles to understand board dynamics and work to improve them

- Use the Styles to assure each board committee has a variety of perspectives
- Use the Styles to better understand the executive director's leadership style and working relationship with the board

governance/nominating committee

Since this committee is the gatekeeper to the board, their work is the number-one way to influence the range of voices at the table. If this committee starts to incorporate the Asking Styles into its understanding of the board now, in three years you will have a more varied board. This committee can:

- Use the Asking Styles to ensure they recruit board members of diverse strengths and perspectives
- Use the Asking Styles to provide new board member orientations that fit each recruit's Style
- Develop a board assessment process that reflects an understanding of various Asking Styles and the impact that has on individual board members' work
- Review the slate of officers through the Styles lens to evaluate in advance what their dynamic will be and whether any changes should be made

board chair & executive director

Your board chair and executive director are the most critical team in the organization. If they can't work together well (and I know this from experience!), it's almost impossible for the organization to do its best work. They can use the Styles to understand each other better and build a better working relationship, as well as to navigate the general board dynamic and the relationship between board members and staff. Here are some topics for discussion:

- What you've learned about yourselves and each other through the Asking Styles and how that might impact your work together going forward

- How you will partner on the next meeting with a funder

- Other key people in the organization and how you might work with them knowing their Style

- How your executive director can help your board chair lead your board given the board's Asking Style composition

full board

You might be reading this book along with your entire board, in which case you're ready for a variety of rich discussions and exercises. If so, you might consider this book's companion workbook, and having the board delve into its exercises. Most exercises are meant for board meetings, though some can be done independently and discussed in group settings.

conclusion

I hope you now feel armed with a new set of tools that will help you be the best board member you can be...as part of an amazing team working together to impact the world.

I hope you now see not only all your amazing strengths, but those of your fellow board members. That you more fully understand why they say what they say and act as they do. That you see how you complement each other.

Perhaps you'll even take the Asking Styles out into the world with you, to see all your thoughts, actions, relationships, and more through the powerful lens of the Styles.

Thank you, Rainmaker, for keeping us focused and striving to accomplish more.

Thank you, Go-Getter, for keeping the passion alive and reminding us we can think big.

Thank you, Kindred Spirit, for reminding us it's all about people, always.

Thank you, Mission Controller, for making sure it can happen and sticking with it until it does.

I must close by thanking you again for being a board member. For giving so much of yourself to make the world a better place. For being a part of our wonderful, quirky nonprofit world.

I wish you all the best.

about the author

Brian Saber, president of Asking Matters™, has spent his entire career asking for money for nonprofits. From his early days as a student leader and telethon caller to his six years in charge of major and principal gifts throughout the Midwest for Brandeis University to his two stints as an executive director, every position has involved significant face-to-face solicitation. He is still honing his asking muscles today, cultivating and soliciting select major donors for a variety of clients.

Brian harnessed all his frontline experience to become a sought-after trainer, coach, and consultant around the country and abroad. His work is transformative. He leads workshops, creates training courses, presents webinars, and coaches top-level staff, taking organizations to the next level.

In a career spent mostly with organizations having budgets under $1 million, Brian is well aware of the fundraising challenges smaller organizations face. He knows most organizations struggle to afford consulting services; they're just not in the budget. With that perspective, Brian co-created Asking Matters to provide resources all nonprofits could afford. This web-based and in-person company trains people how to ask for money and motivates them to do it.

Brian has led training programs and presented at conferences for Prevent Child Abuse America, the Archdiocese of Los Angeles, Social Venture Partners International, National Public Radio, Volunteers of America, the United States Olympic Committee, The Salvation Army, Boys and Girls Clubs of America, AFP International, numerous AFP chapters, the North American YMCA Development Conference, and others.

His first book, *Asking Styles: Revolutionize Your Fundraising*, has become a staple for nonprofit fundraisers and leaders.

Brian lives and works in South Orange, New Jersey. He is the proud father of a 19-year-old son. In his spare time he attends the performing arts, volunteers for numerous organizations, practices yoga, and is immersed in singing lessons, which he started out of nowhere at the age of 54.

about asking matters™

Brian Saber & Andrea Kihlstedt, two experienced fundraising professionals, believed when it came to raising money, the primary limiting factor was people's reluctance to ask for gifts. Andrea, a capital campaign consultant, and Brian, a front-line fundraiser and consultant, decided to develop a set of practical, accessible tools to help staff and board members learn the art and science of asking and find the courage and will to ask.

Through her work on capital campaigns, Andrea knew that when the stakes were high enough to get people to ask, the results were remarkable, with organizations often raising far more money than anyone thought possible. And Brian, a front-line fundraiser who has asked thousands of people for hundreds of millions of dollars of gifts, knew it was possible to overcome one's fears and ask...and ask and ask. He believed that, while it might never get easy and often isn't fun, the results were well worth the discomfort and often yielded much more than money.

In 2009, Brian and Andrea launched Asking Matters, a company that uses web-based learning and in-person training to provide the information and inspiration needed to motivate staff and board members to ask. In 2013 Brian acquired Andrea's share, and he continues to own and run the company today.

acknowledgments

Acknowledging Andrea Kihlstedt never gets old for me. There would be no Asking Matters or Asking Styles without her, and our professional and personal relationships mean the world to me. As a Go-Getter, Andrea creatively and fearlessly comes up with one amazing idea after another, and her impact on the field and on me has been immeasurable.

I want to thank Michael Davidson for his wisdom, partnership, and overall menschiness (if that's a word!). I met Michael almost 20 years ago, and he has taught me an incredible amount about boards over the years. I wouldn't have had the perspective to write this book without Michael.

Many thanks to Tom West, my publisher/editor/friend. He's another great partner from whom I've learned a ton and whose judgment I trust completely.

Thanks to all my wonderful clients. The trainings I provided your boards over these last ten years gave me the deep understanding I needed to write this book.

Though I won't thank COVID-19, I do have to acknowledge it. Being forced to hunker down, by myself, gave me the free time and motivation I needed to write this book. With most of my short-term work cancelled and my beloved performing arts world dark, time was plentiful and I could only do so many jigsaw puzzles (39 as of publication). This book gave me a goal—something to focus on whose accomplishment would help me stay sane during horrific and lonely times.

Last but always most importantly, I thank my son. He rocks my world every day.

—*Brian*

Made in the USA
Columbia, SC
05 October 2024

43663376R00064